Introduction

This student workbook is intended to reinforce your learning of the content on the GCSE Physics specification (J643) from the OCR Gateway Science Suite.

This workbook is cross-referenced to the revision and classroom companion *OCR Gateway GCSE Physics Revision Plus*, published by Letts and Lonsdale.

The pages for each unit are divided into topics to correspond with the specification and revision guide, and provide a clear, manageable structure to your revision. They focus on the material that is externally assessed (i.e. tested under exam conditions). They do not cover the Skills Assessment (Research Study, Data Tasks and Practical Skills), which is marked by your teacher.

The questions and activities are designed to strengthen your understanding of the subject. They are varied in style to keep your study interesting, and there is limited space for each question so you will have to think carefully about your answers.

This workbook is suitable for use by Foundation and Higher Tier students.

> HT Any material that is limited to Higher tier students appears inside a grey tinted box, clearly labelled with the symbol HT.

A Note to Teachers

The pages in this workbook can be used as…

- classwork sheets – students can use the revision guide to answer the questions
- harder classwork sheets – pupils study the topic and then answer the questions without using the revision guide
- easy-to-mark homework sheets – to test pupils' understanding and reinforce their learning
- the basis for learning homework tasks which are then tested in subsequent lessons
- test materials for topics or entire units
- a structured revision programme prior to the objective tests / written exams.

Answers to this workbook are available to order.

Contents

Contents

Heating Houses

1 The temperature of a can of cola that has just been taken out of a fridge is 4°C. The temperature of a freshly made cup of tea is 65°C. Two hours later the temperatures of the cola and the tea are equal. Explain why.

....

....

2 William and Emma decided to carry out an experiment to see how quickly a hot cup of tea cooled over time.

Time (minutes)	Temperature (°C)
0	60
1	47
2	38
3	32
4	27
5	23
6	20
7	19
8	19

a) Plot their results on the graph paper.

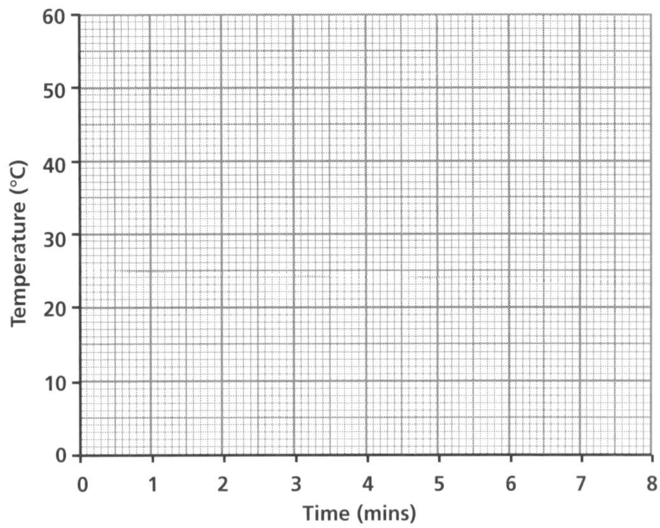

b) Why is the line on your graph steeper at the start of the experiment than at the end?

....

....

c) What was the temperature of the room in which the experiment was carried out? ....

d) Where does all the heat energy given out by the hot tea go?

....

3 State whether the following statements are **true** or **false**.

a) Heat is a measure of how hot something is. ....

b) Heat is a measurement of energy. ....

c) Heat is measured in degrees Celsius. ....

Heating Houses

1 Complete the following sentence:

The amount of energy needed to raise the temperature of an object depends on the change required, the

.... of the object, and the .... heat capacity of the material that the object is made from.

2 An electrical heater in a car provides 200J of heat energy per second. If it is running for 2 minutes, what is the total amount of energy supplied?

3 Below are three statements about specific heat capacity. Only one of them is correct. Tick the box next to the correct statement.

a) The specific heat capacity is the temperature increase in 1kg of a material due to 1J of heat energy. ☐

b) The specific heat capacity is the energy needed to raise the temperature of 1kg of a material by 1°C. ☐

c) The specific heat capacity is the time it takes to raise the temperature of 1kg of a material by 1°C. ☐

HT **4** The specific heat capacity of glass is 700J/kg°C.

a) How many joules of energy are required to raise the temperature of a 2kg sheet of glass by 20°C?

b) 20 000J of heat energy are used to raise the temperature of a 5kg sheet of glass. If the initial temperature of the glass was 20°C, what is the final temperature?

Heating Houses

1 The following graph shows how the temperature of the water in a kettle changes as it boils.

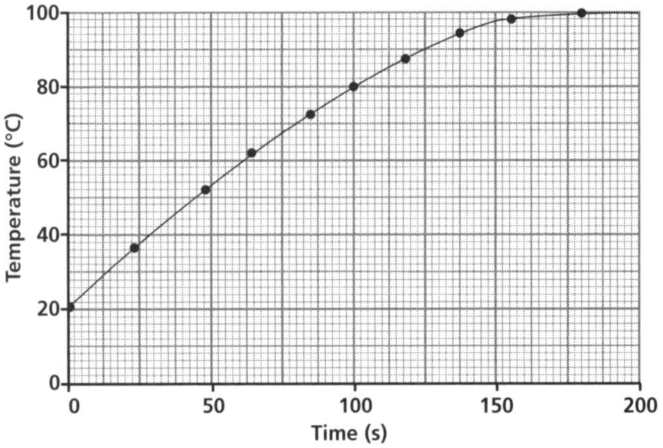

a) The temperature reaches 100°C and then remains constant. Why does this happen?

b) If the kettle remained switched on for another 200 seconds, would the temperature of the water rise above 100°C? Explain your answer.

c) If a far more powerful kettle was used to boil the water, would the water reach a higher temperature? Explain your answer.

2 Read the following sentences about specific latent heat and tick the box next to the statement that is incorrect.

a) The specific latent heat is the amount of energy required to melt or boil 1kg of a material. ☐

b) The specific latent heat is the amount of energy required to raise the temperature of 1kg of a material by 1°C. ☐

c) The specific latent heat depends on the material being heated. ☐

d) The specific latent heat depends on the state of the material. ☐

HT **3** During heating, the temperature of melting ice does not change. Explain where the heat energy goes.

Keeping Houses Warm

1 **a)** Name four good conductors of heat.

i) .... **ii)** ....

iii) .... **iv)** ....

b) Why is it important for the handle of a saucepan to be made from a material such as wood or plastic?

....

2 Gareth and Charlotte have just bought a house. The house has not been insulated. The table below lists parts of the house that may be insulated to reduce energy losses. The cost of each method is also given.

a) Complete the table.

Where Energy is Lost	Method of Insulation	Cost of Insulation (£)	Annual Saving (£)	Payback Time (years)
Roof		300	75	
Walls		800	40	
Windows		3000	100	
Doors		30	20	

b) Which method of insulation would you recommend they install first? Explain your answer.

....

....

c) **i)** Which method of insulation would you recommend they install last? Explain your answer.

....

ii) What are the advantages of installing this method of insulation?

....

3 Trapped air is a very good insulator. Name three everyday items which take advantage of this property.

a) ....

b) ....

c) ....

Keeping Houses Warm

HT **1** Explain how each of the following reduces energy consumption in the home.

a) Cavity wall insulation. ....

b) Draught excluders. ....

c) Roof insulation. ....

d) Double glazing. ....

2 Explain the meaning of…

a) useful energy. ....

....

b) wasted energy. ....

....

3 a) If we say that an electric drill is 60% efficient, what does this mean?

....

b) What happens to the other 40% of the energy? Where does it go, and in what form?

....

4 The table below lists three everyday devices. For each one, write down the useful energy transfer it is designed to bring about and the way(s) in which energy is wasted.

Device	Useful Energy Transfer	Wasted Energy
Television		
Light bulb		
Car		

5 For every 200 joules of energy supplied to a hairdryer, only 80 joules come out as useful energy.

a) How much is wasted? ....

b) Calculate the efficiency of the hairdryer.

....

How Insulation Works

1 Complete the following sentence:

Rooms at the top of a building will have a .... temperature than those lower down.

This is because warm air will .... when allowed to flow and cooler air will

.... to take its place.

HT 2 Name the three methods of transferring heat, and briefly explain how they transfer heat.

a) ....

b) ....

c) ....

3 **a)** Explain why the handle of a brass poker gradually becomes hot if the other end is left in the fire.

....

....

....

b) What should the poker have on the end so that someone can hold it?

....

4 When an electric kettle is switched on it will take a few minutes to heat the water. Explain in detail how the element at the bottom of the kettle heats all of the water.

....

....

....

5 **a)** With reference to colour and texture, which surfaces are good absorbers of radiation?

....

b) Which surfaces are poor emitters of radiation?

....

Cooking with Waves

1 Light is part of a family of waves called the electromagnetic spectrum. The other members of the family are X-rays, ultraviolet, radio waves, infrared, microwaves and gamma rays.

In the table below, arrange the waves in order of their frequency.

Highest frequency						**Lowest frequency**

2 State the uses and dangers of microwave radiation.

Uses: ....

....

Dangers: ....

....

3 Complete the following sentences with the name of the correct type of electromagnetic radiation:

a) .... are used to transmit radio and television programmes.

b) Remote controls use .... rays.

c) .... can be used in medical treatment whereas .... can be used for medical diagnosis.

HT **4 a)** Describe, in your own words, how a microwave oven cooks food.

....

....

b) Describe, in your own words, how an oven which uses infrared radiation cooks food.

....

....

....

Infrared Signals

1 Circle the device below which does not use infrared radiation.

Remote controls **Automatic door sensors** **Microwave ovens** **Burglar alarms**

2 Complete the following sentences.

a) An optical fibre is a long transparent cable with a very .... diameter.

b) The pulses of light or .... radiation are totally internally ....

along the length of the fibre.

c) None of the light is .... because the glass–air boundary acts as a plane

....

3 With the aid of a diagram, explain why a light ray might reflect or refract when passing from glass into air.

4 The diagram shows a length of optical fibre.

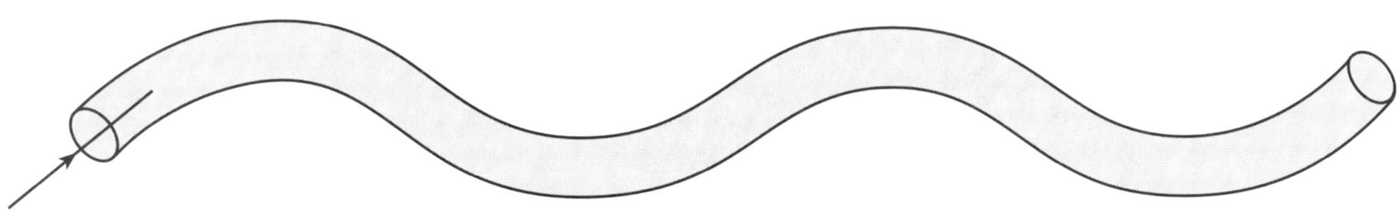

a) Complete accurately the passage of the ray of light through the fibre.

b) What advantages are there in using optical fibres for telecommunications?

Infrared Signals

1 a) What is the difference between analogue and digital signals? Draw diagrams of both to help explain your answer.

Analogue

Digital

b) List three advantages of transmitting information using digital signals rather than analogue signals.

i)

ii)

iii)

2 Explain what multiplexing is.

3 Explain, with the help of a diagram, why interference does not degrade a digital signal but can affect an analogue signal.

1 Explain why wireless technology is used in radios, mobile phones and laptop computers.

....

....

....

2 State which type of wave – **radio wave** or **microwave** – is used by each of the following forms of communication.

a) Mobile phones: .... **b)** Radio broadcasting: ....

c) Television broadcasting: ....

3 Explain why your mobile phone may not work in a mountainous area. Draw a diagram to help you explain your answer.

....

....

....

....

....

....

HT

4 Complete the following sentences.

The electrically charged layer in the Earth's .... is called the .... This layer will reflect .... wavelength .... waves.

5 Explain why the refraction and diffraction of radio waves can cause problems.

....

....

....

Light

1 What type of wave is light? Circle the correct option below.

p-wave **transverse** **longitudinal** **surface**

2 Jean is generating a wave by moving one end of a rope up and down 2 times every second, as shown in the diagram. Jean is 3m away from the wall.

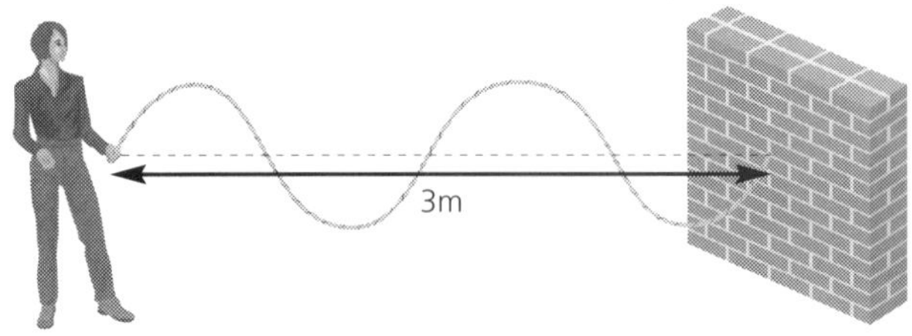

a) What is the frequency of the wave generated?

b) What is the wavelength of the wave generated?

c) The amplitude of the wave is 0.5m. Mark this on the diagram.

3 A wave is travelling at a constant speed. What happens to the frequency of the wave if its wavelength is increased?

4 A wave has a frequency of 300Hz and a wavelength of 10m. Calculate the speed of the wave.

5 A radio station transmits signals at a wavelength of 252m. The speed of radio waves is 300 000 000m/s. Calculate the frequency of these radio waves.

6 The Bay Radio Station transmits on a frequency of 96.9MHz (M = 1 million)

a) What does a frequency of 96.9MHz mean?

HT **b)** The speed of radio waves is 300 million m/s. Calculate the wavelength of these waves.

1 How can modern communication methods be so fast?

2 Explain how messages can be sent using Morse code.

HT

3 Explain, with the help of diagrams, why laser light is so intense.

4 Why is visible light not used for wireless signalling?

5 Why would you choose a low resistance wire to send an electrical signal through?

6 Why can homes in mountainous areas still receive radio signals?

Stable Earth

1 Explain the differences between P-waves and S-waves.

HT

2 The diagram shows the structure of the Earth. An earthquake occurs at point A on the Earth's surface. Two types of shock waves are produced by the earthquake: P-waves and S-waves.

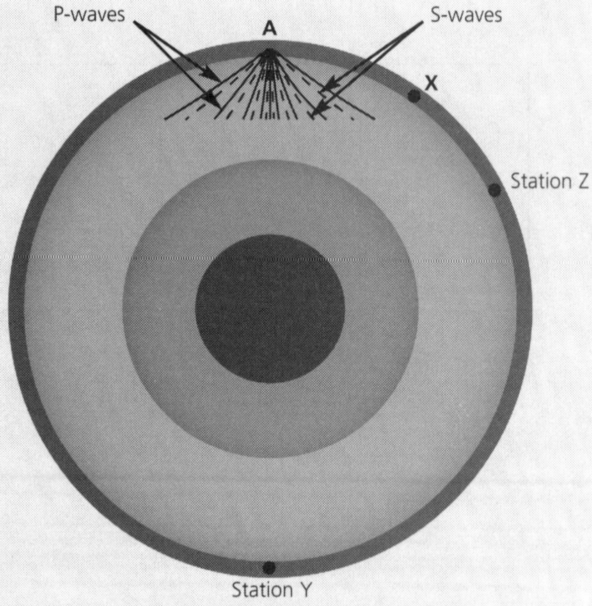

a) Complete the diagram to show the path of the P-waves and S-waves through the Earth.

b) State, with reasons, whether **P-waves** or **S-waves** or **both** will reach...

i) Station Z:

ii) Station Y:

c) Buildings at X were seen to vibrate up and down and then a few seconds later vibrate from side to side. Explain why this was so.

d) What can be deduced about the structure of the Earth from the study of P and S waves?

Stable Earth

1 Which form of electromagnetic radiation can lead to skin cancer?

2 Is the following statement **true** or **false**?

Light-skinned people are at less risk of getting skin cancer because their skin reflects more of the radiation.

3 If the recommended exposure time at midday is 15 minutes, what is the minimum factor sunblock you would have to apply if you wanted to spend 3 hours in the sun?

4 How can you help to reduce the contributing factors to global warming?

HT

5 Why is it so difficult to predict how global temperatures will change over the next 50 years?

6 What reason do some scientists give to explain the rise in the number of people suffering from skin cancer?

Collecting Energy from the Sun

1 Tick the box next to the statement below which is incorrect.

a) The power output of photocells depends upon the area exposed to sunlight. ☐

b) Photocells transfer light into electricity. ☐

c) Photocells produce a direct current. ☐

d) Photocells produce a current which is alternating in direction. ☐

2 List the three main advantages of photocells.

a) ______________________________

b) ______________________________

c) ______________________________

3 What factors might deter a house owner from investing in photocells?

____

____

____

HT

4 Explain how photocells convert the Sun's energy into electric current. Write no more than four bullet points.

- ______________________________
- ______________________________
- ______________________________
- ______________________________

5 Explain why more power is gained when the solar panels track the Sun's position.

____

____

____

____

Collecting Energy from the Sun

1 Explain why the conservatory of a house gets so warm in the summer.

2 What energy change takes place in wind turbines?

3 Would it be fair to refer to wind energy as solar energy? Explain your answer.

HT

4 Visible light passes through glass but infrared light does not. Explain how this accounts for passive heating in the home.

5 Suggest a location where wind turbines would be a good alternative energy source. Explain your answer.

6 Suggest a location where wind turbines would be a poor alternative energy source. Explain your answer.

Generating Electricity

1 Complete the following sentences.

When a metal wire cuts through the lines of .... of the .... field,

a .... is produced in the wire.

Electricity can be generated either by moving the .... or the ....

2 Give three ways in which the generated current can be increased.

a) ....

b) ....

c) ....

3 Explain how the size and direction of an alternating current changes as time passes.

....

....

....

4 Sketch an AC generator and use your sketch to explain why an alternating current is generated in the coil.

....

....

....

....

....

5 Describe the process that produces electricity by burning coal.

....

....

....

HT 6 If an AC current takes 0.02 seconds to complete each cycle, what is its frequency?

....

....

Generating Electricity

1 What is the name given to fuels such as wood, straw and manure?

2 List the three main types of fossil fuel.

a) .... **b)** .... **c)** ....

3 List three dangers associated with nuclear power.

a)

b)

c)

4 What type of transformer would be situated between transmission lines and a town?

5 Explain why most power stations are only about 30% efficient.

HT

6 Why is less energy wasted when electricity is distributed at a high voltage?

7 A small power station produces 400 000J of electrical energy from every 2 000 000J of fuel energy.

What is the efficiency of the plant?

Fuels for Power

1 Tick the box next to the statement below which is correct.

a) An electric current is the energy flowing per unit of charge. ☐

b) An electric current is the resistance to the flow of charge. ☐

c) An electric current is the flow of electric charge. ☐

2 Complete the following sentences.

Electric charge transfers .... from the battery to the components in the circuit.

In a filament lamp, most of the .... energy is transformed into ....

The power of a device is determined by the rate of .... transfer.

3 A battery provides 12V to a complete circuit resulting in a current of 4A. What is the power supplied?

....

....

....

HT

4 The current flowing through a 60W bulb is 0.25A. What is the voltage?

....

....

5 A 5V battery is supplying energy to a circuit at a rate of 10J/s. What is the current in the circuit?

....

....

6 Imagine you work at an electricity company. Write down some reasons you could give to your customers to convince them to use off-peak electricity.

....

....

....

....

1 The table shows the power rating of different electrical appliances and how long they are switched on for each week. Complete the table. (Electricity costs 8p per kWh.)

Appliance	Power Rating (kW)	Time Used Each Week	Energy Transferred (kWh)	Cost per Week
Kettle	1.5	6h		
Immersion heater	3.0	5h		
Cooker	4.0	15h		
Electric fire	2.0	30h		
Hairdryer	0.75		3	
Iron		2h	2	
Washing machine	2.5	6.5h		
Tumble dryer	2.0			8p
Electric shower		3h		192p

2 Fred decided to check his electricity meter reading because his last two bills had only been estimates.

The previous estimated meter reading was 34215. The present meter reading is shown alongside.

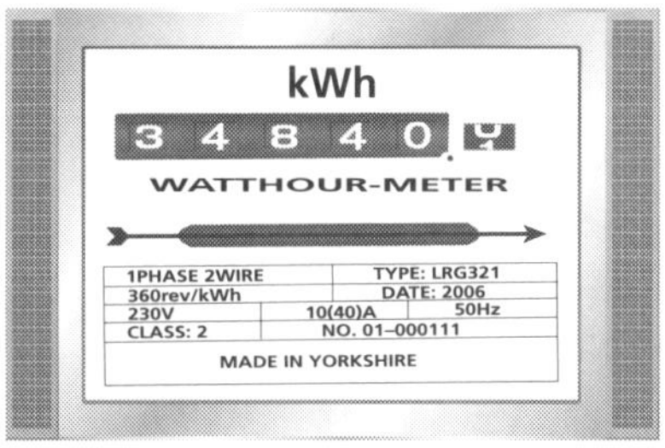

a) How many units of electricity has Fred used since the last statement?

b) If electricity costs 8p per unit, how much does Fred owe the electricity company?

HT 3 An air-conditioning unit is supplied with 2.5kW of electrical energy over a two-hour period. What is its power rating?

Fuels for Power

HT 1 Discuss the advantages and disadvantages of biomass from an environmental perspective.

2 What factors may deter a business from investing in renewable sources of energy?

3 The cost of nuclear fuel is relatively low. Does this mean it is a cheap form of energy production? Explain your answer.

4 Why might a government be reluctant to move away from using fossil fuels?

Nuclear Radiations

1 What do we mean if we say a substance is radioactive?

2 **a)** Below are the three main types of radiation and a list of descriptions. Draw lines between the boxes to match the radiation to the correct description. The descriptions can apply to more than one ionising radiation.

Descriptions	Radiation	Descriptions
Emitted from the nucleus.	α	Very short wavelength radiation.
Passes through air and paper but absorbed by a few millimetres of aluminium.	β	Fast-moving electron.
Very high frequency radiation.	γ	Absorbed by a thin sheet of paper.
Consists of two protons and two neutrons.		Has a positive charge.
		Helium nucleus.

b) Why does the emission of gamma radiation have no effect on the structure of the nucleus?

3 People who handle radioactive materials should take certain safety measures. Write down four of them.

a)

b)

c)

d)

4 Explain why it is more expensive to dispose of high-level waste than low-level waste.

HT 5 Which of the problems associated with dealing with radioactive waste may be of most concern to the government? Explain your answer.

Nuclear Radiations

1 The diagram alongside shows a simple smoke detector. Explain what happens if smoke enters the space between the electrodes.

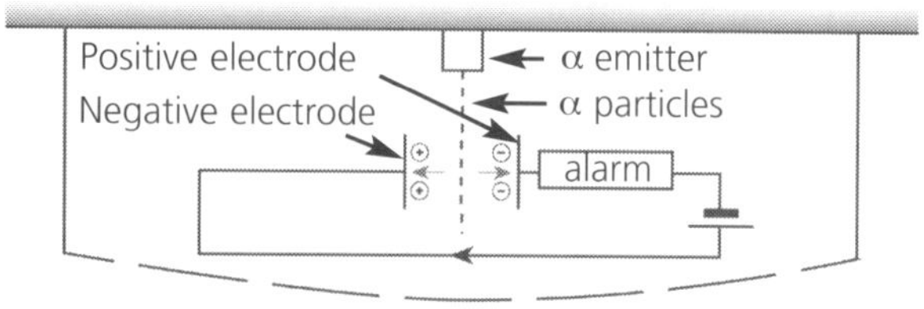

2 The diagram alongside shows a method of controlling the thickness of steel at a steel mill. A radioactive source which emits gamma radiation is placed on one side of the steel and a radiation detector on the other.

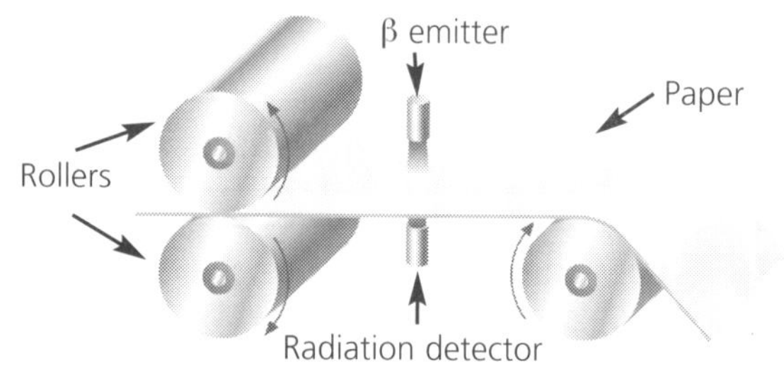

a) How will the amount of radiation reaching the detector change as the steel gets thicker?

b) What effect will this have on the distance between the rollers?

c) Explain, in detail, why a radioisotope which emits alpha or beta particles could not be used for this job.

d) Explain, in detail, why a radioisotope which emits gamma rays is used for this job.

3 Radiation can be used to sterilise medical instruments.

a) What type of radiation would be used for this job?

b) How do the instruments become sterile?

c) What is the advantage of sterilising the instruments in this way, rather than heating them or treating them with chemicals?

4 Radiation emitted from a radioactive material is often called ionising radiation.

Explain what is meant by the word 'ionising'.

Our Magnetic Field

1. Why is the Earth's magnetic field important for life on this planet?

....

....

2. Tick the box next to the statement below which is incorrect.

a) Clouds of charged particles ejected by the Sun are called solar flares. ☐

b) Moving charged particles produce magnetic fields. ☐

c) Solar flares produce very strong magnetic fields. ☐

d) Solar flares dangerously disrupt the Earth's gravitational field. ☐

3. Solar flares can interfere with the operation of satellites. Write down three problems that this could cause on Earth.

a) ....

b) ....

c) ....

4. In the space below, draw the magnetic field pattern around a current-carrying coil of wire.

HT

5. What causes the Aurora Borealis?

....

....

....

....

Exploring our Solar System

1 Circle the objects below that do not give out their own light.

Planets **Comets** **Meteors** **Stars**

2 What is the force that causes the planets to orbit the Sun?

3 List the three biggest planets in the Solar System.

a) **b)** **c)**

4 In the space provided below, sketch a planet in an elliptical orbit around a star.

5 Explain the differences between comets and meteors.

HT 6 Describe how a comet's orbit around the Sun differs from the Moon's orbit around the Earth.

Exploring our Solar System

1 **a)** Imagine you are an engineer building a rocket for a manned space mission to Pluto. What are the difficulties you would have to take into account?

b) If you were an astronaut, which of the difficulties you have listed for part a) would be of most concern to you?

2 Why might an unmanned space mission be a better solution?

HT

3 Tick the box next to the correct definition of a light year.

a) The speed of light. ☐

b) The distance light travels in one year. ☐

c) The average speed of light over a whole year. ☐

4 Why would it be advantageous to have a human on a space mission?

Threats to Earth

1 Where can asteroids normally be found?

2 What are the possible consequences of an asteroid colliding with the Earth?

3 Asteroids have collided with the Earth many times in the past. The following statements are all facts. Tick the box next to the fact that cannot be used as evidence to support this idea.

a) There are layers of unusual elements found in rocks. ☐

b) Craters can be found all over the planet. ☐

c) Tectonic plates are constantly sliding past each other. ☐

d) Fossils suggest the sudden death of many animals. ☐

4 I have a core of frozen gas and come from far beyond the planets. I have a highly elliptical orbit and gain speed as I approach the Sun. What am I?

5 What does **NEO** stand for in physics?

HT

6 What is the force that causes comets to speed up and slow down?

7 What measures can we take to prevent a collision between Earth and a comet or asteroid?

1 Complete the following sentences.

The .... theory states that the Universe started .... of years ago in one huge ....

Every .... in space is moving away from us.

HT 2 How do physicists estimate the age and starting point of the Universe?

3 What evidence do we have to suggest that there was a big explosion?

4 Explain what is meant by 'red shift'.

5 Why is the light from more distant objects red-shifted more than light from closer objects?

The Big Bang

1 In the space provided, illustrate the final stages in the life of a medium-weight star.

2 How might this cycle differ for a star many times larger than our Sun?

3 Space is black, so how can we see black holes?

HT

4 What is the difference between a neutron star and a black hole?

5 Summarise the formation of a star into four (or fewer) bullet points.

1 Calculate the average speeds of each of the following:

a) A car that travels 120km in 3 hours.

b) An aeroplane that flies 3600km in 5 hours.

c) A runner who takes 3 min 20s to complete a 1500m race.

d) A world-class sprinter who runs 100m in 9.8s.

2 A walker covers 6km in 1 hour. What is her average speed in metres per second? (Make sure you use the correct units.) Show your workings.

HT

3 A car travels at an average speed of 100km/h.
How far would it travel in $2\frac{1}{2}$ hours? Show your workings.

4 A coach drives from London to Leeds, which is a distance of 200 miles. The coach averages a speed of 60mph for the first 50 miles, 50mph for the next 90 miles and 40mph for the remainder of the journey. How long does it take the coach to travel from London to Leeds?

5 A jet aircraft travels at an average speed of 550mph. It takes 570 minutes to get to its destination. How far away is the destination? Show your workings.

Speed

1 Jim and Dom were having an 800m race. Their times were recorded every 100m. The table below shows the results.

Distance Run (m)	100	200	300	400	500	600	700	800
Jim's Time (s)	15	30	45	65	85	105	130	155
Dom's Time (s)	20	40	60	80	95	110	125	140

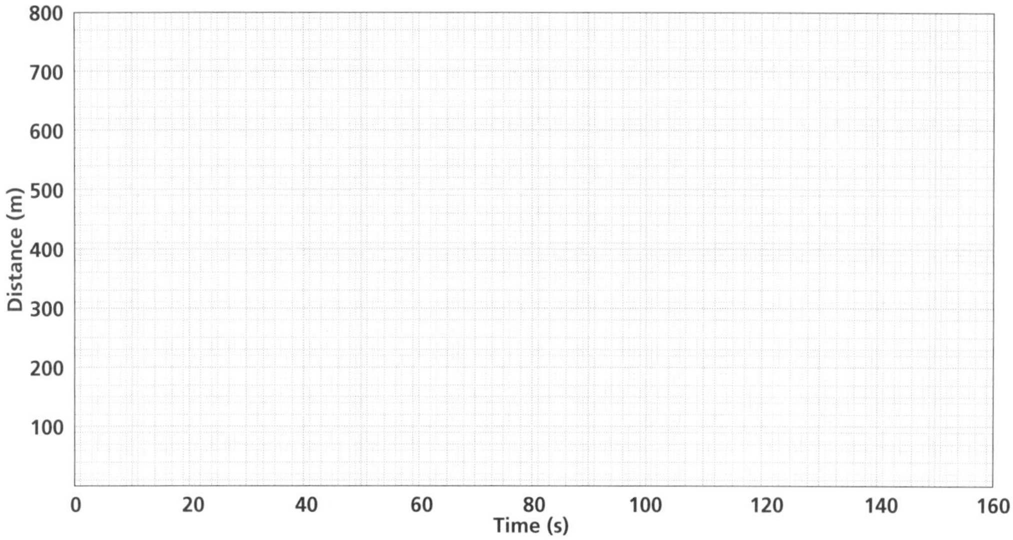

a) Draw the distance–time graphs for both boys' results on the axes above.

b) Between which two times was Jim's speed the slowest? ....

c) Between which two times was Dom's speed the slowest? ....

d) Who won the race and by how many seconds? ....

2 In the space below, sketch a distance–time graph showing a car accelerating at a constant rate from rest.

1 **a)** What do we mean by the term 'acceleration'? ....

b) What units is acceleration measured in? ....

c) What do we mean by the term 'deceleration'? ....

2 Calculate the acceleration for each of the following. (Show your workings, and make sure you use the correct units.)

a) A car that accelerates uniformly from rest to a speed of 15m/s in a time of 5s.

....

....

b) A train that accelerates uniformly from rest and reaches a speed of 30m/s after 15s.

....

....

c) A car that accelerates from a speed of 20m/s to 34m/s in 4s.

....

....

d) A train that accelerates from rest and reaches a speed of 40m/s after 2 minutes.

....

....

3 A fighter plane lands on an aircraft carrier at a speed of 40m/s. It is stopped in a time of 2s. Calculate the deceleration of the fighter plane.

....

HT

4 A car is travelling at 12m/s. It accelerates at a rate of $2m/s^2$ for 10 seconds. Calculate its new speed. Show your workings.

....

....

....

5 An object at rest falls from the top of a cliff. It falls through the air with an acceleration of $10m/s^2$ and hits the ground at a speed of 24m/s. How long did it take the object to reach the ground?

....

....

Changing Speed

1 The table below shows a motorcyclist's speed at regular intervals as he travels between two sets of traffic lights.

Time (s)	0	2	4	6	8	10	12	14	16	18	20	22
Speed (m/s)	0	5	10	10	10	13	16	16	12	8	4	0

a) Draw a speed–time graph of the motorcyclist's journey on the axes opposite.

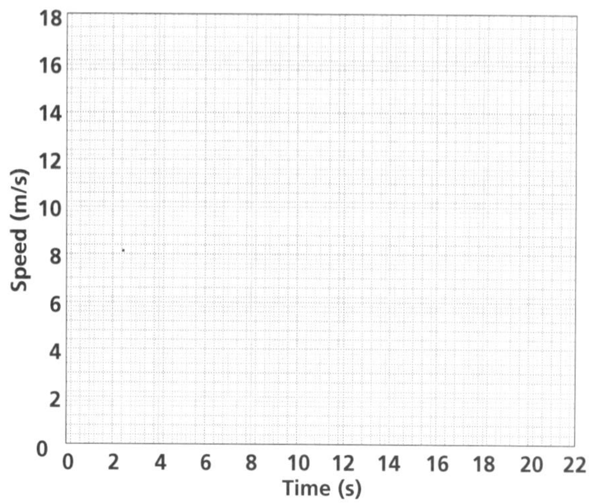

b) Between which two times was the motorcyclist's acceleration the greatest?

Between .... and ....

c) Between which times was the motorcyclist's speed constant?

Between .... and ....

Between .... and ....

HT **2** The speed–time graph below is for a train moving from one station to the next.

a) Describe the motion of the train.

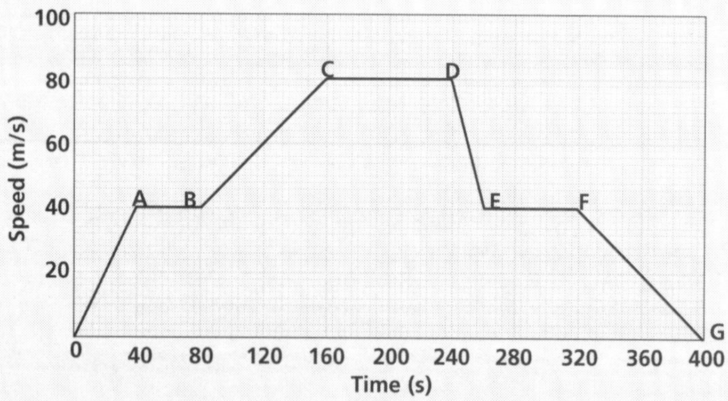

....

....

....

b) Calculate the two accelerations of the train.

....

....

c) Calculate the two decelerations of the train.

....

....

d) Calculate the total distance travelled by the train.

....

Forces and Motion

1 Diagrams A to F show the forces acting on three cars and three lorries.

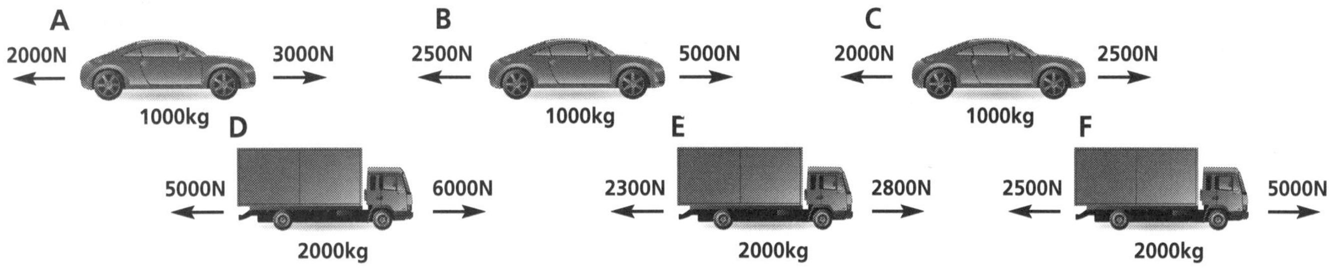

For each of these questions, explain your answer.

a) Which car has the smallest acceleration? ....

b) Which lorry has the greatest acceleration? ....

c) Will car B or lorry F have the greater acceleration? ....

d) Which two vehicles have the same acceleration? ....

2 A car is moving along a straight road. The total mass of the car is 250kg.

a) The car is moving at a constant speed of 20m/s. The value of the driving force is 2000N. What is the value of the resistive force? Explain your answer.

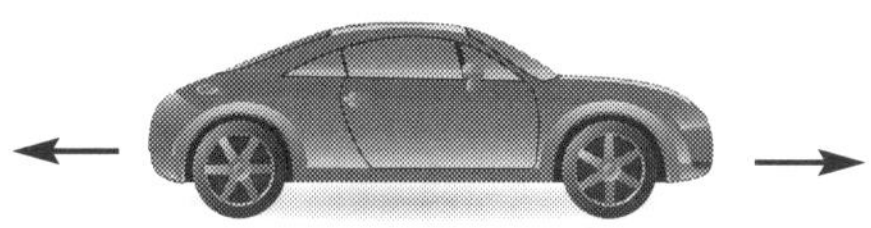

....

....

b) The car increases speed from 20m/s to 30m/s in 5s. Calculate the acceleration of the car.

....

c) Calculate the force needed to produce the acceleration in part b) above. ....

....

d) What is the total force produced by the car during this acceleration? ....

3 A car decelerates from 15m/s to a standstill in 5s. The mass of the car and the driver is 1000kg. Explain how the force required to produce the same deceleration would change if the mass of the car and driver was increased to 1500kg.

....

Forces and Motion

1 The stopping distance of a vehicle depends on two factors: the distance travelled during the driver's thinking time and the distance travelled during the time the brakes are applied.

a) If a driver's reaction time is 0.75s and the car is travelling at 12m/s, calculate how far the car travels before the driver presses his foot on the brake.

....

....

b) Once the brakes have been pressed it takes another 6 seconds for the car to stop. Calculate the deceleration of the car.

....

....

2 **a)** List three factors that can increase thinking distance.

i) .... **ii)** .... **iii)** ....

b) What effect does an increase in thinking time have on…

i) braking distance? ....

ii) overall stopping distance? ....

3 List three factors that can increase braking distance.

a) .... **b)** .... **c)** ....

HT 4 Draw lines between the boxes to match the changed factor to the effect it has on braking distance.

Changed factor	Effect
A larger force is applied to the brake pedal.	Braking distance is increased.
Less force is applied to the brake pedal.	Braking distance is reduced.
It starts raining.	
The vehicle has more passengers in it.	
The vehicle is travelling slower.	

1 Only one of the activities below does not involve doing work. Circle it.

Weight training **Riding a bike** **Standing on top of a tall tower** **Eating lunch**

2 Why should we be concerned if more people buy more powerful cars?

3 A cyclist moves along a flat road against a resistive force of 100N. If the cyclist travels 1000m, calculate how much work he has done.

4 Matt cycles a distance of 2000m against a resistive force of 150N. He travels this distance in 400s.

a) Calculate how much work is done by Matt.

b) What is Matt's power output?

5 A pumped storage system is used to store water in a dam. Water flows down through the pipes, turning turbines which generate electricity. When there is not much demand for electricity, the water is pumped back up to the top reservoir.

Calculate the work done in pumping 10 000N of water from the lower reservoir through a distance of 100m to the upper reservoir.

HT

6 The power output of a crane is 1.6kW. Calculate how long it will take to lift a load of 5000N through a distance of 8m.

Energy on the Move

1 a) What is kinetic energy? ....

b) A truck of mass 2000kg and a car of mass 1000kg are travelling down a motorway at the same speed.

i) Which one has the greatest kinetic energy? ....

ii) Explain your answer. ....

c) Two cars of the same mass are travelling down a road. Explain how one car could have more kinetic energy than the other.

....

....

2 For the following pairs of objects, state which has the most kinetic energy and give a brief reason why:

a) A car of mass 1000kg or a lorry of mass 3200kg, both moving at 10m/s.

....

b) Car A of mass 100kg moving at 15m/s or Car B of mass 1000kg moving at 10m/s.

....

3 Why is it not fair to say that electric cars reduce pollution?

....

....

HT

4 Calculate the kinetic energy of the following:

a) A car of mass 1000kg moving along a road at a constant speed of 20m/s.

....

....

b) A truck of mass 32 000kg moving along a road at a speed of 10m/s.

....

....

c) A skier of mass 90kg skiing down a hill at a speed of 15m/s.

....

....

d) A toy truck of mass 1300g moving at a speed of 30cm/s.

....

....

Crumple Zones

1 Seatbelts and air bags reduce the deceleration of the car in an accident. Is this statement **true** or **false**?

2 Explain why the following safety features are included in cars:

a) seatbelts

b) air bags

c) brakes

d) crumple zone

3 Why would the passenger section not be part of a car's crumple zone?

4 What is the difference between active and passive safety features in cars?

5 Explain the advantages of anti-lock braking systems over normal brakes.

6 Which passive safety feature do you think prevents the most accidents? Explain your choice.

HT

7 The stopping forces experienced by a passenger during a crash can be reduced by increasing the collision time. Choose a safety feature which performs this task and describe how it works.

Falling Safely

1 When terminal speed is reached, which two forces are balanced?

a) .... **b)** ....

2 A skydiver of weight 700N steps out of a plane.

a) What causes the skydiver to fall? ....

b) When the skydiver steps out of the plane she initially accelerates. Explain, in terms of the forces acting on the skydiver, why she accelerates.

....

c) What happens to the weight of the skydiver as she falls? ....

d) What will happen to the value of the air resistance as she falls? Why does this happen?

....

e) Eventually the skydiver will fall at a steady speed. Explain, in terms of the forces acting on the skydiver, why she falls at a steady speed.

....

....

f) Eventually, after she has reached a terminal speed, the skydiver opens her parachute. What effect will this have on the air resistance acting on her?

....

3 The table below shows the speed of a skydiver at 5-second intervals after she steps out of a plane, up to the point where she opens her parachute.

Time (s)	0	5	10	15	20	25	30	35	40	45	50
Speed (m/s)	0	10	19	27	33	36	38	39	40	40	40

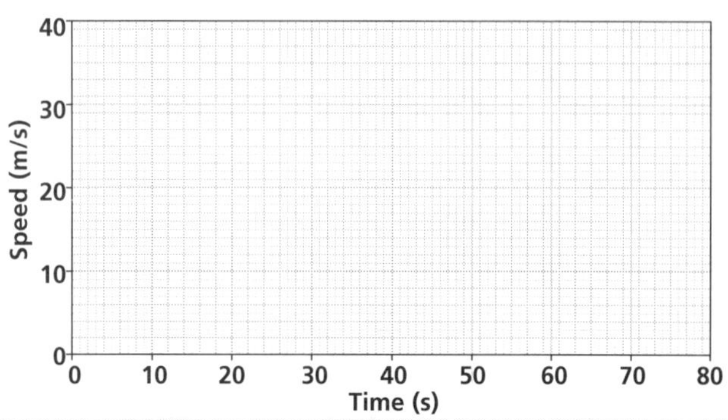

a) Draw a speed–time graph of the falling skydiver on the axes opposite.

b) The skydiver eventually comes to a rest on the ground after 78s. On the axes opposite complete the graph, showing how her speed might change after 50s (when she opens her parachute).

The Energy of Games and Theme Rides

1 **a)** What is gravitational potential energy?

....

b) Give two examples of objects that have gravitational potential energy.

i) .... **ii)** ....

2 The diagrams alongside show a ball on a slope.

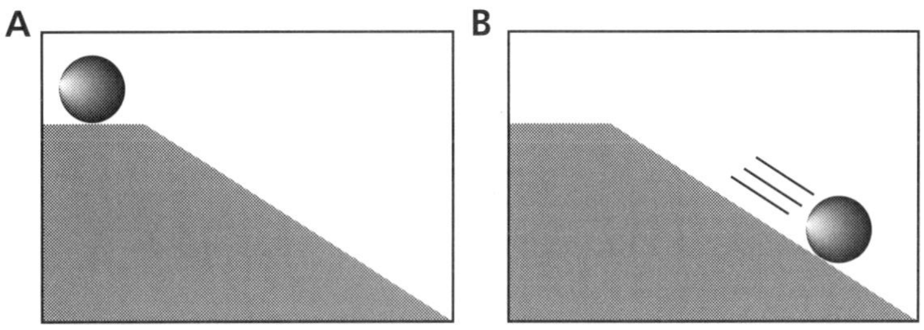

a) Which type of energy does the ball have when it is stationary at the top of the slope in diagram A?

....

b) Which types of energy does the ball have when it is rolling down the slope in diagram B?

....

HT

3 A cyclist climbs from a height of 100m to a height of 300m. The cyclist has a mass of 70kg. By how much does the cyclist's gravitational potential energy increase? (Remember: formula, workings and unit.)

....

....

4 An electric motor of power rating 4000W lifts a load of 400N. It takes 10s to lift the load.

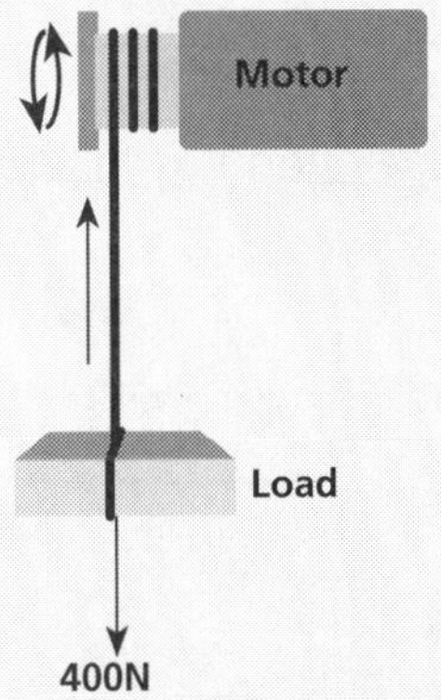

a) What is the main energy change that is taking place?

....

b) If the motor is 100% efficient, how much energy does the motor transfer to the load? (Remember: formula, workings and unit.)

....

....

c) What height is the load lifted through? (Remember: formula, workings and unit.)

....

The Energy of Games and Theme Rides

1 In the space below, sketch the shape of a roller-coaster in which the following energy changes take place:

- First, there is a gradual transfer of electrical energy to gravitational potential energy.
- This gravitational potential energy is then swiftly transferred into kinetic energy.
- The kinetic energy remains constant for a period of time before transferring back into gravitational potential energy again.

2 If a roller-coaster designer wishes to increase the maximum kinetic energy of the cars, which should he double: their mass or the speed? Explain your answer.

....

....

3 If you moved a roller-coaster ride to the Moon, how would the ride be different and why?

....

....

HT

4 Explain how the kinetic and gravitational potential energy of an object may vary when it is falling at its terminal speed.

....

....

5 Some masses are shown below. Calculate their weight on Earth. ($g = 10m/s^2$ or $10N/kg$)

a) Mass = 2kg .... **b)** Mass = 10kg ....

....

1 Describe a situation where the build up of static electricity may lead to an explosion.

....

....

....

2 List three situations where static electricity is a nuisance but not a danger.

a) ....

b) ....

c) ....

3 Hugh did an experiment in which he charged up two polythene rods and one Perspex rod by rubbing them with a cloth. The charge on the rods is shown in the diagram below.

Polythene rod rubbed with a cloth — Perspex rod rubbed with a cloth

a) He suspended the charged Perspex rod and one of the charged polythene rods. He then moved the other charged polythene rod towards the suspended rods.
Complete the sentences below to describe what would happen...

i) when he brought the charged polythene rod close to the suspended charged Perspex rod

....

ii) when he brought the charged polythene rod close to the suspended charged polythene rod.

....

b) What can we conclude from this?

....

HT

c) Explain how the rods became charged.

....

Uses of Electrostatics

1 Rearrange the following statements to describe how a photocopier works.

A Charged impression of the plate attracts tiny specs of black powder.
B Paper is heated to fix the final image.
C Copying plate is electrically charged.
D Powder is transferred from the plate to the paper.
E Image of the page to be copied is projected onto the plate.
F Charge leaks away due to light, leaving an electrostatic impression of the page.

☐ ☐ ☐ ☐ ☐ ☐

2 Describe, in detail, how a laser printer works.

....

....

....

3 How can static electricity be used to help someone whose heart has stopped?

....

....

4 Fitting dust precipitators to a chimney causes most of the dust to collect at the bottom of the chimney rather than escaping into the atmosphere. Describe how this works.

....

....

5 Bicycles can be painted using an electrostatic paint spray. The paint is given a positive charge.

a) What charge should the bike be given? Explain your answer. ....

....

b) What is the advantage of using this method? ....

....

....

1 The diagram shows a circuit breaker.

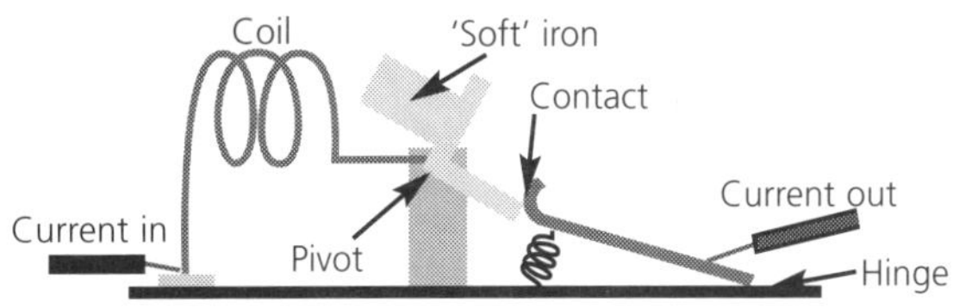

a) What is the job of a circuit breaker?

....

....

b) What is the advantage of having a circuit breaker rather than a fuse?

....

....

2 Describe what might happen if a fault occurs in an electrical appliance that is being used without a fuse or a circuit breaker.

....

....

....

3 How does a fuse work?

....

....

....

HT

4 a) The diagram shows a hairdryer that has a plastic casing. The hairdryer plug only has two wires. Which two wires does it have?

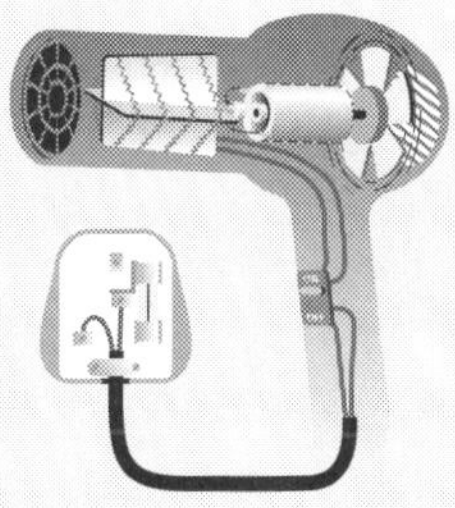

i) .... ii) ....

b) Which of the usual three wires is missing?................................

c) The hairdryer is safe to use without the third wire. Explain why.

....

....

Safe Electricals

1 Indicate whether the following statements are **true** or **false**.

a) The colour of the earth wire is blue. ....

b) The neutral wire carries current away from an appliance. ....

c) Appliances with outer metal cases have no earth wire. ....

d) The live wire carries current to the appliance. ....

e) All appliances have cables with three wires in them. ....

f) A fuse is always part of the live wire. ....

2 What does the term 'double insulated' mean? ....

....

HT

3 The diagram alongside shows a toaster with a stainless-steel casing.
The earth wire is connected to the outer casing of the toaster.

a) What is the purpose of the earth wire? ....

....

b) If the brown live wire became loose and touched the outer casing of the toaster, explain how the earth wire would make the appliance safe.

....

....

c) What would have happened if the earth wire was not connected to the outer casing of the toaster?

....

d) Why don't double-insulated appliances need to be earthed? ....

....

e) Why are double-insulated appliances still protected by a fuse?

....

1 What is resistance?

2 The circuit below is used to measure the resistance of a fixed resistor.

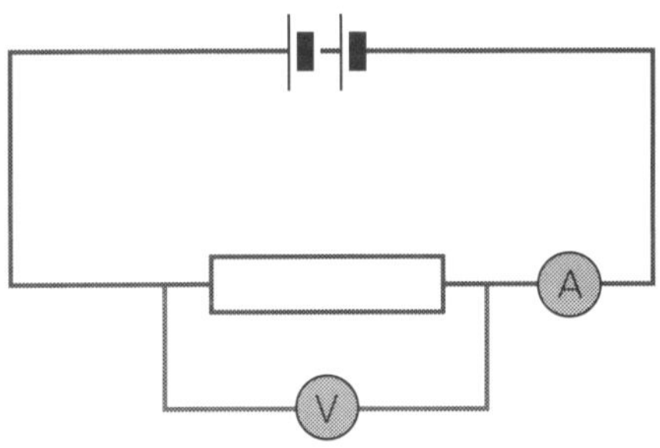

a) The reading on the voltmeter is 6V and the reading on the ammeter is 1.5A. Calculate the resistance of the resistor.

b) What would happen to the readings on the voltmeter and ammeter if one of the cells was removed? Explain your answer.

c) A different resistor was placed in the circuit. When the potential difference is 6V, the current flowing is 0.2A. Calculate the resistance of the resistor.

HT

3 For the circuits shown below, each cell provides a potential difference of 1.5V. The total resistance of two resistors in series is simply their resistance added together. Complete the table below:

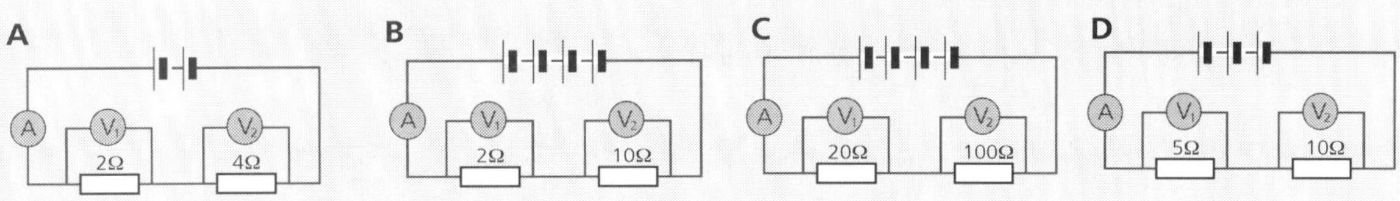

	Circuit A	Circuit B	Circuit C	Circuit D
p.d. supplied				
Total resistance				
Ammeter reading				
V_1				
V_2				

Ultrasound

1 One of the statements below is not true. Put a tick in the box to indicate which one.

a) Ultrasound is high-frequency sound waves. ☐

b) Ultrasound travels at the speed of light. ☐

c) Ultrasound has a frequency greater than 20 000Hz. ☐

d) Humans cannot hear ultrasound. ☐

2 Use the terms below to label the diagram.

Amplitude
Wavelength

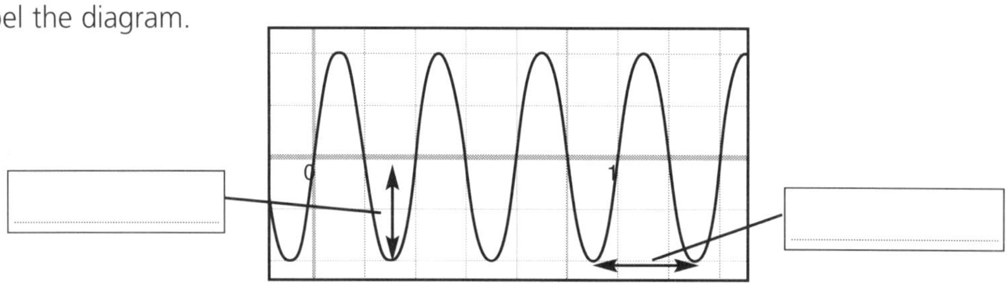

3 Ultrasound scanning has reduced the need for some operations in hospitals. Why is this so?

HT 4 How can ultrasound be used to remove kidney stones without opening up the patient?

5 Why are ultrasound waves used for pre-natal scanning?

HT 6 Using no more than four bullet points, explain how ultrasonic waves are used to build up a picture of the inside of the body.

HT

1 Give two advantages of ultrasound over X-ray imaging.

a) ....

b) ....

2 How are ultrasound waves used to create an image?

....

....

....

3 a) Complete each diagram to show the way a slinky spring would behave if it is vibrated by someone's hand in the directions shown.

i)

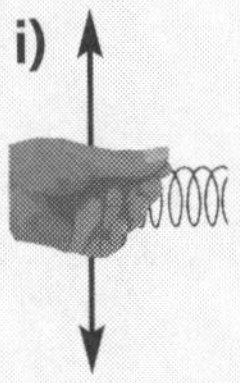

ii)

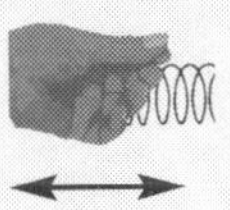

b) On the longitudinal wave you have drawn, label where rarefaction and compression occur.

c) What type of wave is a) ii)?

....

d) Describe the movement of the particles in this wave.

....

....

e) Which of the waves generated in the above models could represent a light wave?

....

f) Draw on diagram a) ii) the movement of one particle in the wave.

Treatment

1 List three similarities between X-rays and gamma rays.

a) ……

b) ……

c) ……

2 Rearrange the following word to reveal the name of the person in a hospital who takes X-rays.

PRODIHERRAGA ……

3 Describe two ways in which gamma rays can be used in hospitals.

a) ……

b) ……

HT

4 When electrons lose energy very quickly they emit electromagnetic radiation. Why are very high-speed electrons required to produce X-rays?

……

5 Explain why a nucleus may emit gamma radiation.

……

6 **a)** Gamma rays can be used to kill cancer cells. Explain, in as much detail as possible, how this process is carried out.

……

b) Gamma rays can also be a danger to health. Explain why.

……

What is Radioactivity?

1 Name the three types of radiation.

a) ....

b) ....

c) ....

2 Put a tick in the box(es) next to the correct statement(s) below.

a) Radioactivity comes from the nucleus of an unstable atom. ☐

b) Radioactivity decreases with time. ☐

c) Radioactivity is measured by the total number of decays a material emits. ☐

HT

3 Complete the following sentences using the words below:

element **neutrons** **atomic** **protons** **mass**

After alpha emission, the new atom will have 2 fewer .... and 2 fewer ....

The .... number will have decreased by 2 and the .... number by 4.

The new atom is a different ....

4 After beta emission, the mass number of the atom remains the same, even though it becomes a new element. How is this so?

....

....

....

5 **a)** Radon-220 will decay into polonium-216. What kind of emission is this? Explain why.

....

....

b) Radon has an atomic number of 86. Use the information given in part a) to calculate the atomic number of polonium.

....

....

What is Radioactivity?

HT

1 A radioisotope emits beta particles only. It has a half-life of 2 days.

Originally there is 200g of the active isotope. What mass of the isotope will remain radioactive after…

a) 2 days? ....

b) 4 days? ....

c) 8 days? ....

d) 16 days? ....

2 The table below shows the activity of a radioactive substance against time:

Time (mins)	0	2	4	6	8
Activity (Bq)	48	24	12	6	3

a) Draw a graph of activity against time.

b) What is the half-life of this radioactive substance?

....

3 Americium-241 is used in smoke detectors. It has a half-life of 460 years.

a) Why is it important for americium-241 to have a long half-life?

....

b) How long would it take americium-241 to decrease to one eighth of its original number of radioactive atoms?

....

4 Uranium isotopes decay to produce stable isotopes of lead. A sample of igneous rock is found to contain seven times as much lead as uranium. The half-life of uranium is 700 000 000 years. Calculate the age of the rock.

....

....

....

....

Satellites, Gravity and Circular Motion

1 Give an example of a natural satellite.

....

2 What force provides the centripetal force that keeps satellites orbiting the Earth?

....

3 What does the term 'orbital period of a satellite' describe?

....

4 Satellites in low polar orbit can be used for imaging the Earth's surface.

a) Explain why they can be used for this purpose.

....

....

....

....

b) Give two other uses of satellites that have a low polar orbit.

i) ....

ii) ....

5 **a)** Describe the motion of a satellite in geostationary orbit.

....

....

b) Give two uses for satellites in geostationary orbit.

i) ....

ii) ....

6 Give two uses for satellites that have not already been given.

a) ....

b) ....

Satellites, Gravity and Circular Motion

HT **1 a)** What happens to the strength of the gravitational field between two objects as they become further apart?

....

b) Explain why the planets further away from the Sun take longer to orbit it.

....

....

....

2 Explain why satellites in low polar orbit take a shorter time to orbit than geostationary satellites do.

....

....

....

3 Complete the table to explain the differences between the orbit of a comet and the orbit of a satellite.

	Difference	Satellite	Comet
a)	What object it orbits	**i)**	**ii)** ....
b)	Shape of orbit	**i)**	**ii)** ....
c)	Speed	**i)**	**ii)** ....

4 Explain why a comet speeds up as it approaches the star it orbits, and slows down as it moves away from it.

....

....

....

....

....

Vectors and Equations of Motion

1 a) What is the difference between a scalar and a vector quantity?

b) Write down whether each of the following terms is a **scalar** or a **vector** quantity.

i) Velocity

ii) Speed

iii) Energy

iv) Force

v) Mass

2 It takes Josh 5 minutes to walk 600 metres. What is his average speed?

3 A car travels from home to the city centre. It takes 10 minutes to travel the first 5km, and 10 minutes to travel the next 1km because of traffic jams. What is the average speed for the journey in m/s?

4 a) You are following a car travelling at 40km/h. You decide to overtake, and accelerate to 50km/h. What is your relative speed as you overtake the car?

b) As you overtake, you see another car coming towards you travelling at 40km/h. What is your relative speed compared with the car travelling towards you?

Vectors and Equations of Motion

1 Shelley is riding her motorbike at a speed of 40m/s. She accelerates at $5m/s^2$ for 3 seconds.

a) What is her final speed?

b) What distance did she travel during the 3 seconds that she was accelerating?

HT

2 If an object has two forces of 3N and 4N acting on it at right angles to each other, what is the resultant force acting on the body?

3 A car travels at 30m/s and then accelerates at $5m/s^2$ to a speed of 45m/s. What distance has the car travelled while accelerating?

4 Another car travels at 30m/s and accelerates at $3m/s^2$ to a speed of 60m/s, taking 10 seconds to accelerate. How far has it travelled while accelerating?

1 A large rock is kicked off the top of a high cliff and falls into the sea. Choose from the words below to complete the following sentences.

Decreases **Increases** **Stays the same**

a) As the rock falls, its vertical velocity ....

b) As the rock falls, its horizontal velocity ....

2 Tick the boxes next to examples of projectile motion.

a) A football kicked into the air. ☐

b) A model aeroplane flying. ☐

c) A dart thrown towards a board. ☐

d) A bullet one second after it is fired from a gun. ☐

HT

3 A cricket ball is thrown off the edge of a cliff into the sea. It is thrown horizontally with a speed of 5m/s. The cliff is 45m high. The acceleration due to gravity is $10m/s^2$.

a) How long does it take for the ball to hit the sea?

....

....

b) How far away from the edge of the cliff is it when it hits the sea?

....

....

....

c) What is the size of its velocity when it hits the sea?

....

....

....

....

....

....

Momentum

1. Write down whether the following statements are **true** or **false**.

   a) When a lorry crashes into a car, the lorry feels the same force as the car.

   b) When you jump off a wall, gravity is pulling the Earth up towards you with the same force that you are being pulled towards the Earth.

   c) When you hit a tennis ball, the racket feels less force from the ball than the ball feels from the racket.

2. Momentum is calculated from two factors. What are they?

   a) **b)**

3. Calculate the momentum of a car of mass 750kg travelling at 12m/s.

4. Calculate the momentum of a bullet of mass 50g travelling at 300m/s.

5. Explain how each of the following safety mechanisms in modern cars reduces injury to the passenger if there is a crash.

   a) Airbags

   b) Crumple zones

Momentum

HT

1. A snowball that has a mass of 500g is thrown at 2m/s. It hits a wall and stops in 0.2 seconds. What force does the snowball exert on the wall?

2. A bullet is fired from a rifle at a speed of 300m/s. The bullet's mass is 50g and the rifle's mass is 5kg. What is the velocity of recoil of the rifle?

3. Explain how a rocket firing in space will propel the rocket backwards.

Satellite Communication

1 a) What is the ionosphere and what effect can it have on radio waves?

b) Explain the other two effects that the Earth's atmosphere can have on radio waves.

i)

ii)

2 a) Give two similarities between microwaves and radio waves.

i)

ii)

b) Give one difference between microwaves and radio waves.

3 a) What does '3MHz' mean?

b) How many waves per second arrive at a receiver from a 3MHz wave?

4 a) What is diffraction?

b) Describe two situations that can cause waves to diffract.

i)

ii)

c) When does maximum diffraction occur?

5 Explain why a satellite dish, instead of an aerial, is needed to pick up satellite television signals.

HT **1** Explain how the size of a gap affects the extent to which radio waves and microwaves are diffracted.

2 Why is only a thin beam of microwaves used to transmit information?

3 Describe what happens when a long wavelength radio wave encounters a hill.

4 **a)** Explain what amplitude modulation of radio waves is.

b) Use the following words to label the diagrams showing the amplitude modulation of a wave.

Signal wave **Carrier wave** **Modulated wave**

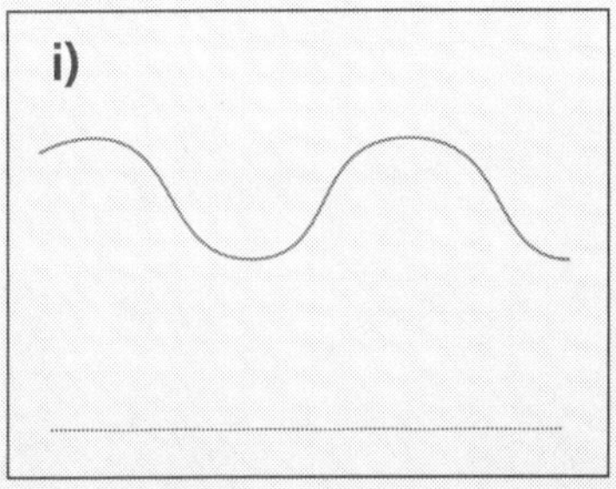

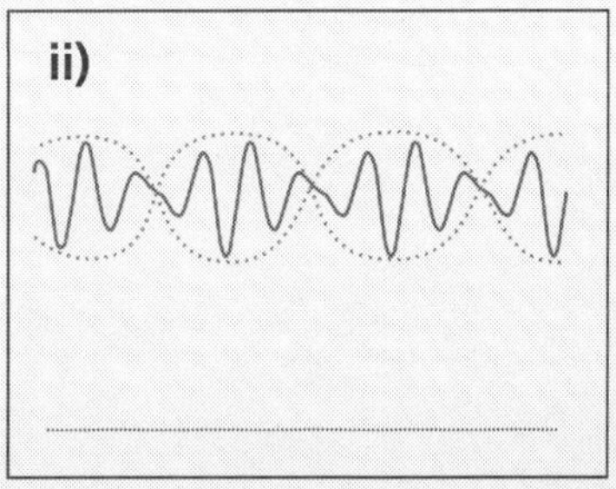

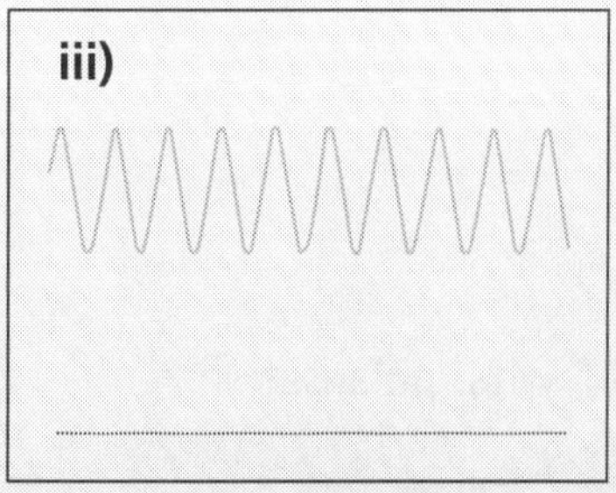

Nature of Waves

1 a) What is 'refraction' of a light wave?

b) Draw a diagram to show light refracting through a glass block.

2 Explain each of the following terms that relate to waves.

a) Interference:

b) Reinforcement:

c) Cancellation:

3 a) Describe the effect you might hear when two sound waves interfere.

b) Describe the effect you might see when two light waves interfere.

4 Explain what polarisation is.

HT **1** For each of the following terms, **i)** explain what it means, and **ii)** draw a diagram to show the effect.

a) Constructive interference **ii)**

i) ____________________

b) Destructive interference **ii)**

i) ____________________

2 Describe and explain the effect of a path difference of half a wavelength when two identical light rays from the same source arrive at a screen.

____

3 Explain how polarising sunglasses work.

____

Refraction of Waves

1 a) Complete the diagrams to show the path of the light ray as it enters and leaves a glass block from air.

i)

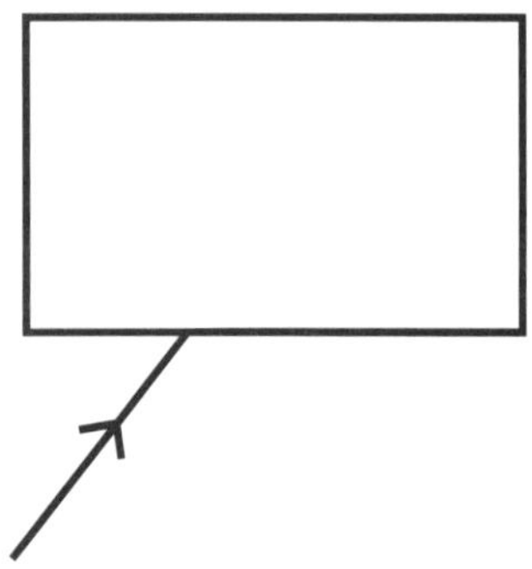

ii)

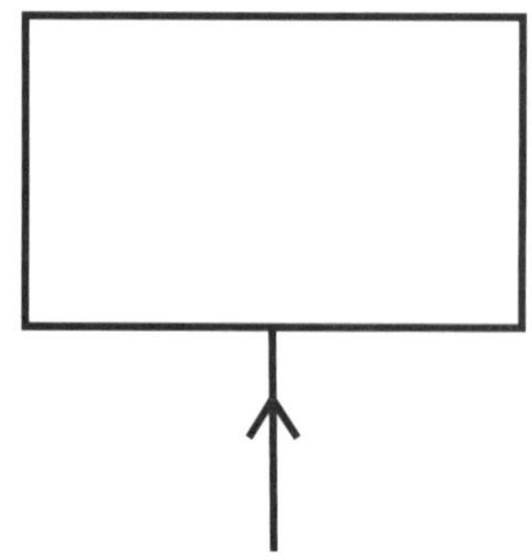

b) On diagram i) above, label the following:

i) Refracted ray

ii) Incident ray

iii) Angle of refraction

iv) Angle of incidence

v) Normal

2 A material has a refractive index of 1.5. What does this mean?

....

....

3 a) What is the 'critical angle' of a material?

....

....

b) What happens if light is travelling at more than the critical angle?

....

....

4 a) Complete this diagram to show what happens to white light as it travels through a prism. Label your diagram clearly.

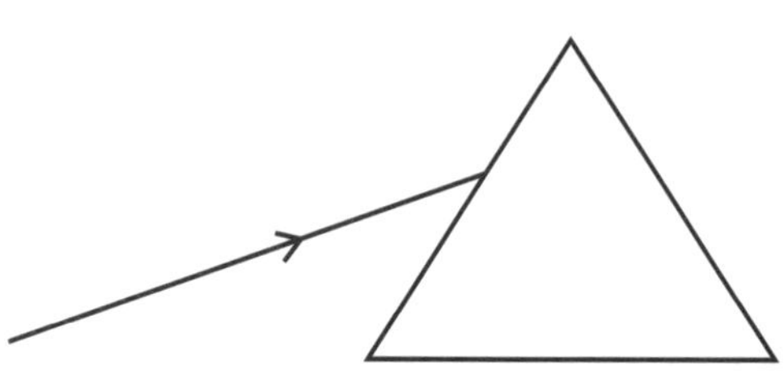

b) Explain how this effect happens.

....

....

....

....

HT **1** The diagrams below show the path of light as it travels through different media.

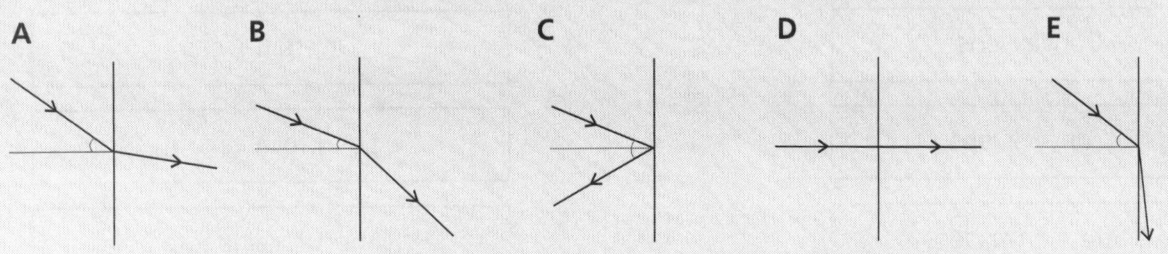

For each situation listed below, choose the diagram that best shows the effect.

a) Light being refracted as it emerges from glass. ....

b) Light being totally internally reflected. ....

c) The critical angle for light in glass. ....

2 Draw lines between the boxes to join the correct pairs.

Large critical angle	Large refractive index
Small critical angle	Small refractive index

3 Write down what happens to each of the features of light, when light travelling in air enters a material such as water.

a) Frequency: ....

b) Wavelength: ....

c) Velocity: ....

4 Light travels through a material that has a refractive index of 1.5. Calculate the angle of refraction if the angle of incidence for light entering the material is 45°.

....

....

....

....

Optics

1 Draw lines between the boxes to connect each lens with its description.

Convex lens	Diverging lens
Concave lens	Long focal length
Fatter convex lens	Short focal length
Thinner convex lens	Converging lens

2 Draw a diagram to show what happens to three rays of light travelling parallel to the axis of a convex lens.

3 Draw a diagram to show what happens to three rays of light travelling parallel to the axis of a concave lens.

HT 4 An object is placed 20cm away from a convex lens that has a focal length of 10cm. Draw a ray diagram to show what happens to the light from the object as it travels through the lens to form an image. Then explain whether the image is real or virtual.

Resisting

1 Under each circuit symbol shown below, write down the name of the device it represents.

a) 

....

b) 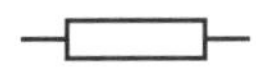

....

c) 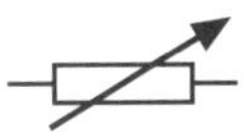

....

d) 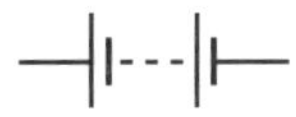

....

e) 

....

f) 

....

2 Name three things that a variable resistor can vary.

a) ....

b) ....

c) ....

3 Complete the table to show the values, units and symbols used when working with electricity.

	Value	Unit	Symbol used in Equations
a)	Voltage		
b)		Amps	
c)			Ω

4 A voltage of 12 volts creates a current of 2 amps in a wire. Calculate the resistance of the wire.

....

....

....

HT **5** A hairdryer powered by 230 volts has a resistance of 7.5 ohms. What current is needed to operate the hairdryer?

....

....

6 Use Ohm's Law to complete the table.

	Voltage (volts)	Current (amps)	Resistance (ohms)
a)	12	3	....
b)	....	5	15
c)	4	....	20

7 The graphs opposite show how the resistance of two devices changes as voltage increases.

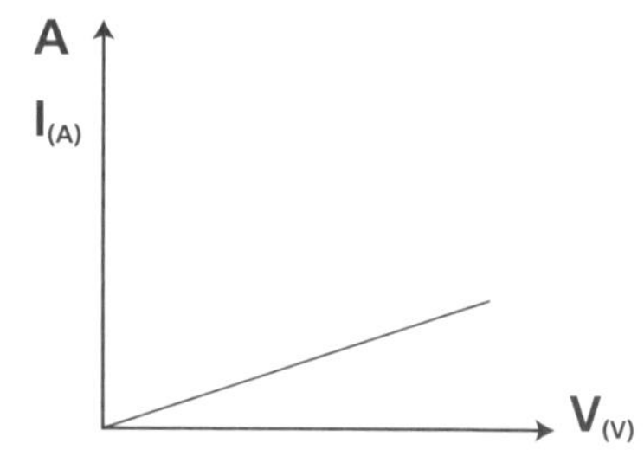

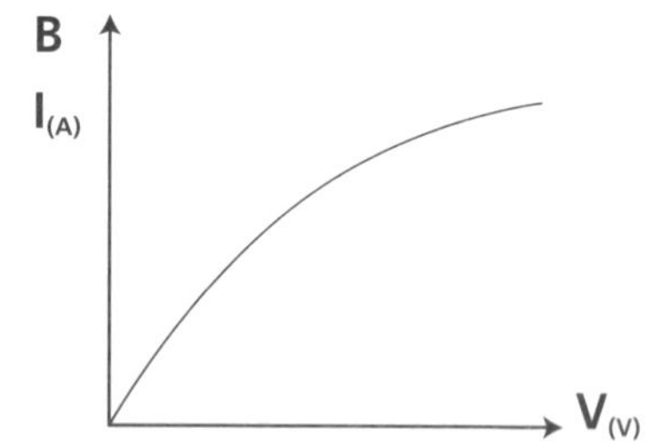

a) For each graph, explain what it shows about the resistance of the device as the voltage is increasing.

i) Graph A: ....

ii) Graph B: ....

b) Suggest one reason to explain why Device A's graph is different to Device B's graph.

....

HT **8** **a)** What would happen to the current in the circuit when a longer wire of the same material is put into the circuit shown? Explain your answer.

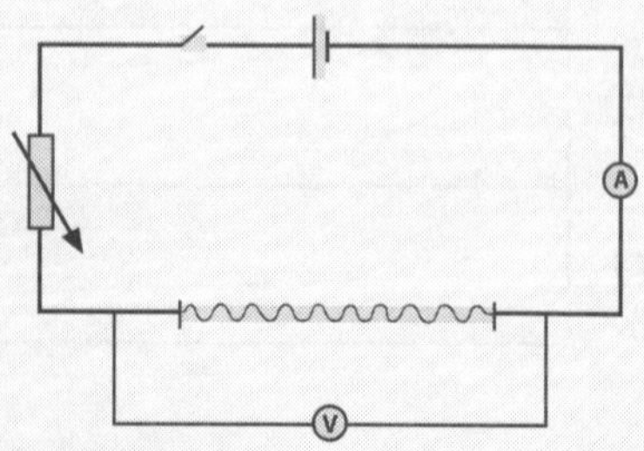

....

....

b) What would happen to the current in the circuit if the wire in the circuit were to get hotter? Explain your answer.

....

....

1 a) What is the name of the device shown opposite?

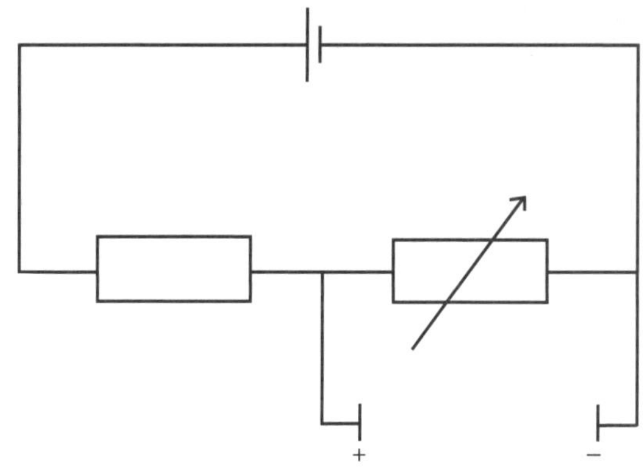

b) Give one advantage of using variable resistors in this type of device.

2 What happens to the resistance of an LDR in a circuit when it is kept in the dark, compared with when it is illuminated?

3 How can the resistance of a thermistor be reduced?

HT

4 a) Explain what happens to the output voltage of the device shown if the circuit is put into the dark.

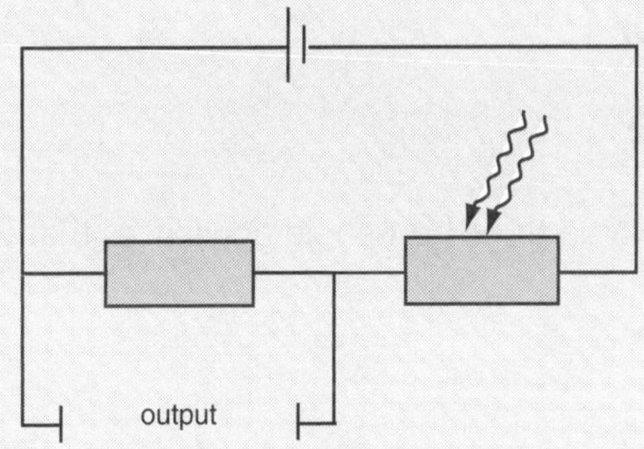

b) Explain what happens to the output voltage in the device shown if the circuit is put into a very hot area.

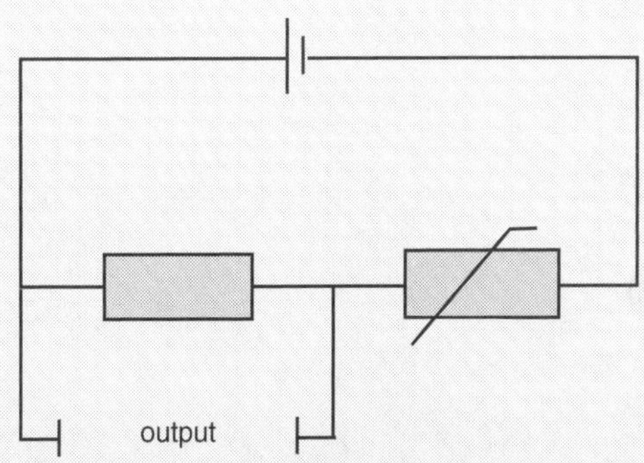

Motoring

1 Diagrams of three magnetic fields are shown below.

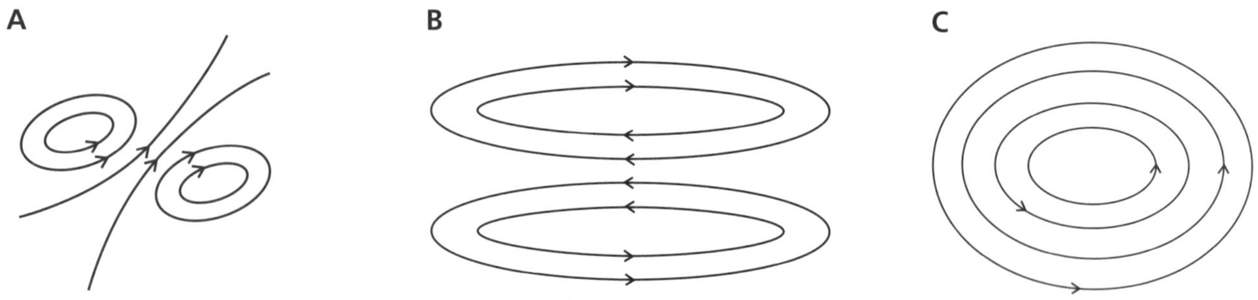

a) Which diagram shows the magnetic field produced by a current in a solenoid? ....

b) Which diagram shows the magnetic field produced by a current in a straight wire? ....

c) Which diagram shows the magnetic field produced by a current in a rectangular coil? ....

2 A current is generated when a magnet is moved near a coil of a wire. What three things can be done to increase the current generated?

a) ....

b) ....

c) ....

3 Name three household appliances that use electric motors.

a) ....

b) ....

c) ....

4 A flat coil of wire is placed in a magnetic field and a current is made to flow through it to make a motor. The flat coil rotates. What three things can be done to increase the speed at which it rotates?

a) ....

b) ....

c) ....

HT **5** Use Fleming's Rule to work out in which direction the wire will move in the following diagrams, and tick the correct box to show the direction of movement.

a)

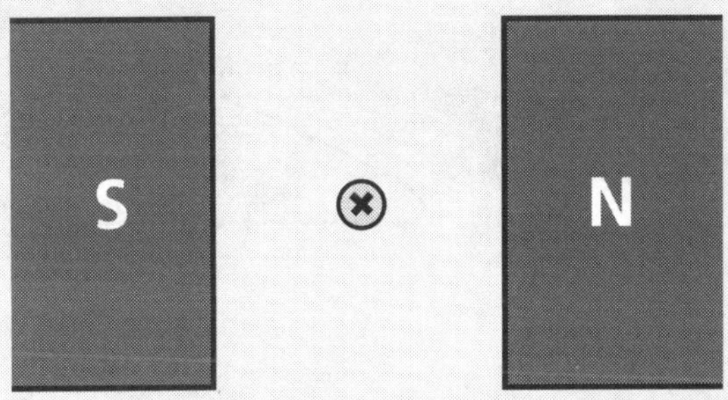

(⊗ indicates current going down the wire)

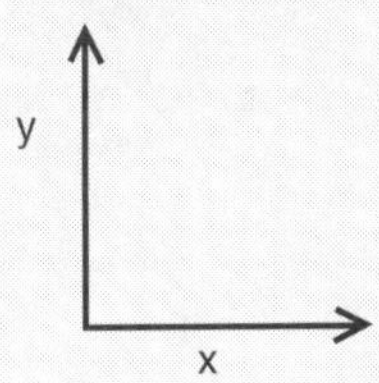

Direction x ☐

Direction y ☐

b)

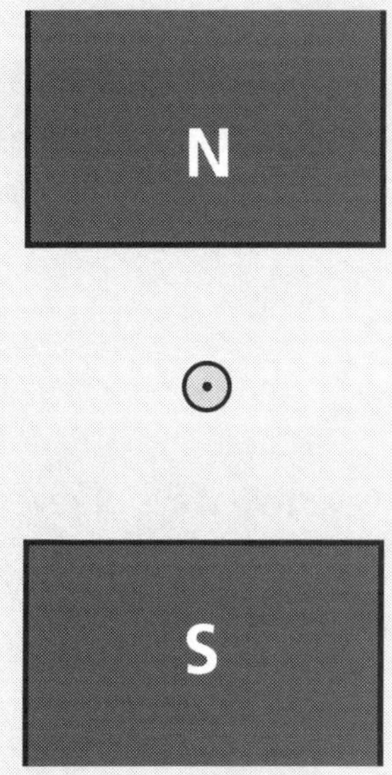

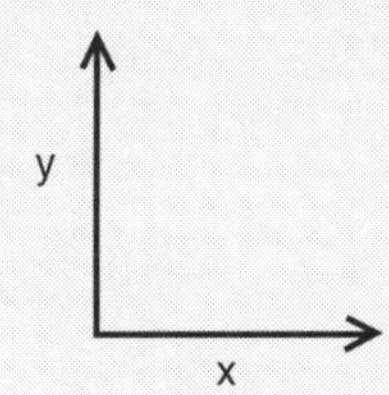

(⊙ indicates current going up the wire)

Direction x ☐

Direction y ☐

6 **a)** What effect does the direction that the current travels in have on the coil in a DC motor?

....

b) What does a split ring commutator do in a DC motor?

....

c) Why is a split ring commutator used in a DC motor and a continuous slip ring used in an AC motor?

....

7 Explain why curved pole pieces are used in real-life motors.

....

....

Generating

1 What is the 'dynamo effect'?

2 a) The diagram shows a wire in a magnetic field. What would happen as the wire is moved upwards and then held still?

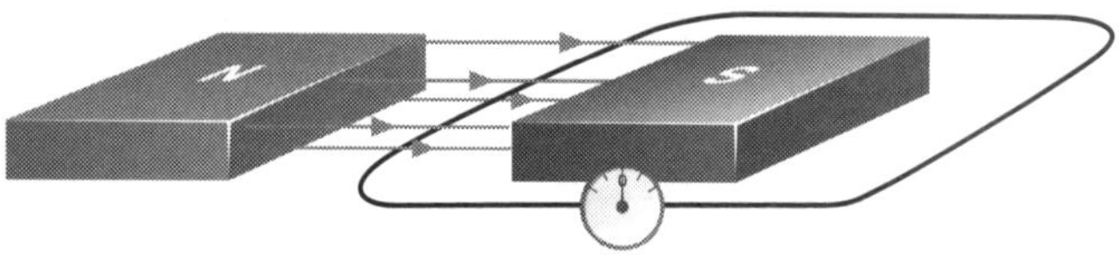

b) Give two ways of reversing the direction of the voltage induced in the wire.

i)

ii)

HT 3 Use the words below to label the diagram of a DC motor.

Field **Force** **Split ring commutator** **Current in** **Current out**

a)

b)

c)

d)

e)

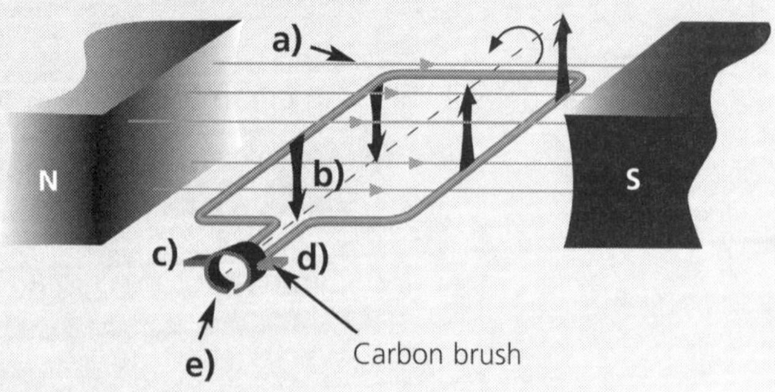

4 If you induce a voltage in a wire by moving it close to a magnetic field, name three ways in which you can induce a larger voltage.

a)

b)

c)

5 Power stations use AC generators. What does AC stand for?

6 a) Give two effects of increasing the speed that an electromagnet rotates in a power station.

i) ....

ii) ....

b) What will happen if the number of turns on an electromagnet's coils is increased?

....

HT 7 The diagram shows an AC generator. Explain how it works. Include in your explanation the effect of the slip ring and brush system.

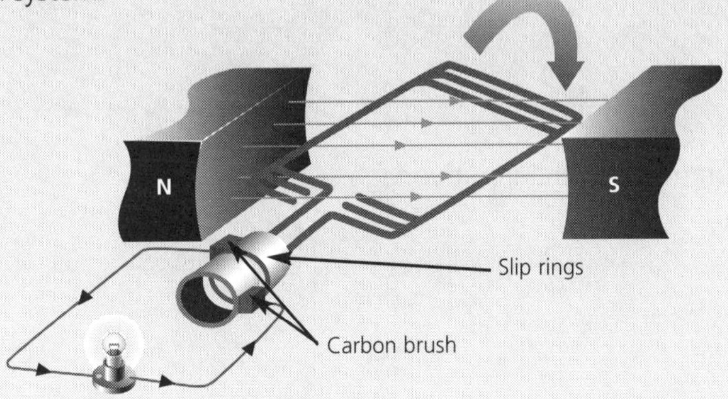

....

....

....

8 Explain the difference between the current output from a split ring commutator in a DC generator and the current output from slip rings and brushes. Include a diagram of the current generated in each case.

....

....

....

....

....

Transforming

1 a) What effect does a step-up transformer have on an AC electrical voltage?

b) What effect does a step-up transformer have on a DC electrical voltage?

2 Explain how step-up and step-down transformers differ in terms of…

a) the number of coils.

b) the output voltage compared to the input voltage.

3 A transformer has 200 turns on the primary coil and 1000 turns on the secondary coil.

a) Is this a step-up or a step-down transformer?

b) The input voltage to the transformer is 12 volts. What is the output voltage?

HT 4 Explain in detail how a voltage is induced in the secondary coil of a transformer.

HT **5** A transformer has an input voltage of 240V, and an output voltage of 12V. Calculate the output current if the input current is 0.5A.

6 **a)** What are transformers used for in the national grid?

b) Explain where in the national grid system each type of transformer is used, and why:

i) Step-up transformers:

ii) Step-down transformers:

7 **a)** Why are isolating transformers used?

HT **b)** Describe how an isolating transformer is different from a step-up or step-down transformer.

8 Why is it an advantage for electricity to be transmitted across the country at a higher voltage than that used in homes?

Charging

1 a) Draw the symbol for a diode in the box.

b) What effect does a diode have on current?

....

....

2 The graph below shows alternating current. On the axes, draw the wave that is produced when AC has passed through a diode and undergone half-wave rectification.

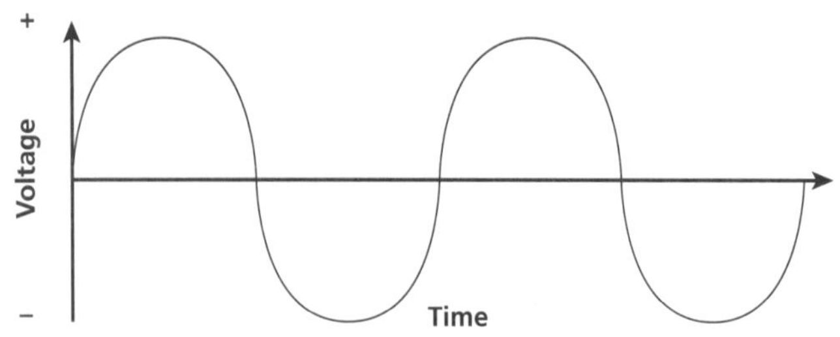

3 Four diodes connected in a bridge rectifier circuit can give full-wave rectification. On the axes below, draw what happens to the alternating current after it has passed through the bridge rectifier.

4 a) Draw the symbol for a capacitor in the box.

b) What does a capacitor do?

....

....

HT **5** A capacitor is charged up, and then connected across a conductor. Explain in detail what happens next.

....

....

....

6 What is the main use for a capacitor in a circuit carrying alternating current?

....

HT **1 a)** Silicon can be doped in two different ways to be used in diodes. What are the two types of silicon called?

i) ______________ **ii)** ______________

b) How are they different?

____

c) What happens to the charge carriers in a silicon diode when it is reverse biased in the circuit?

____

____

2 The graph opposite shows the characteristic curve for a diode. Explain what this curve shows about the resistance of the diode when it is forward biased and when it is reverse biased from the way that current flows through the diode.

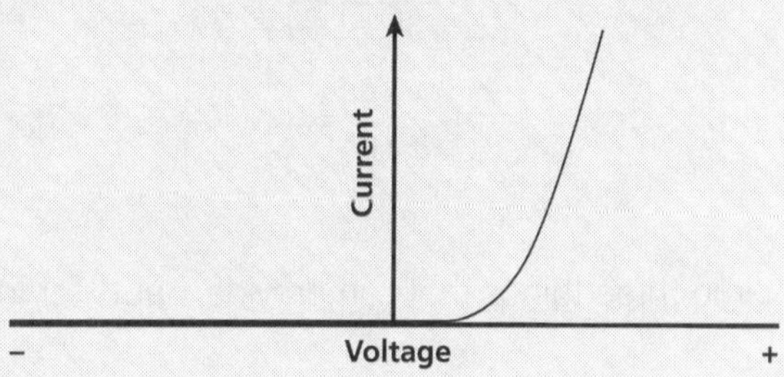

____

____

____

____

____

____

3 The graph shows how the current flowing from a charged capacitor through a conductor changes over time. Explain why the curve is the shape it is.

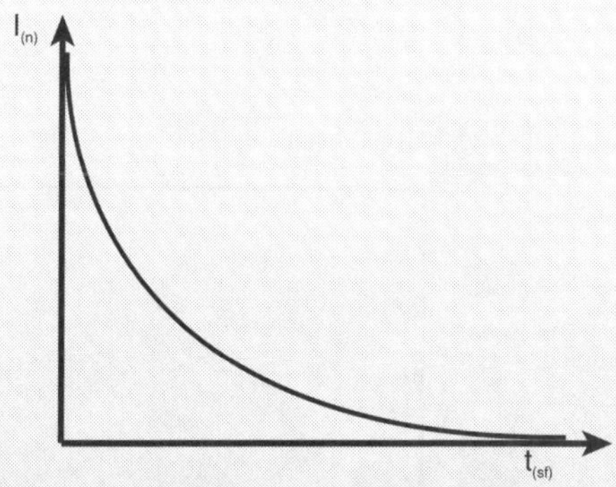

____

____

____

____

____

It's Logical

1 For each of the logic gates shown below **i)** state what it is called, and **ii)** complete the truth table.

a)

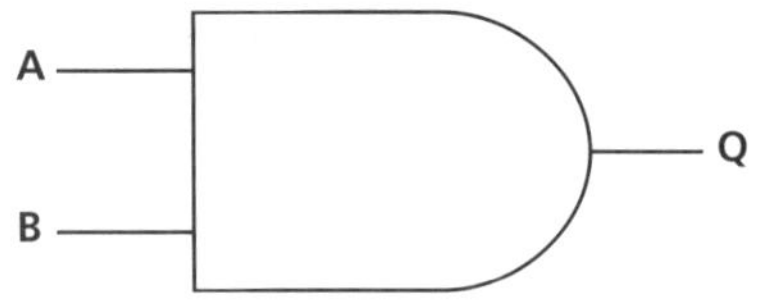

i) ....

ii)

A	B	Q

b)

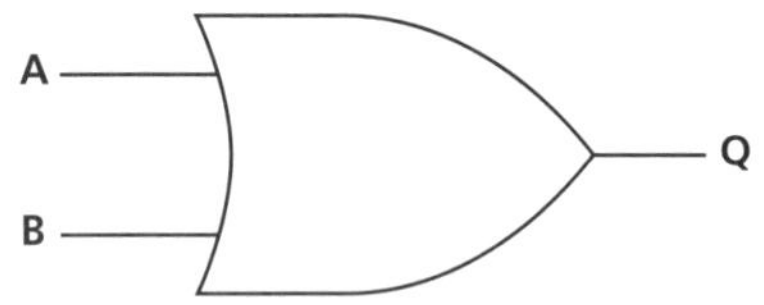

i) ....

ii)

A	B	Q

2 Name three things that can provide inputs for logic gates.

a) .... **b)** .... **c)** ....

HT 3 **a)** For a NAND gate...

i) draw the symbol.

ii) create the truth table.

A	B	Q

b) For a NOR gate...

i) draw the symbol.

ii) create the truth table.

A	B	Q

1 A combination of logic gates is shown below. Construct the truth table for this combination of logic gates.

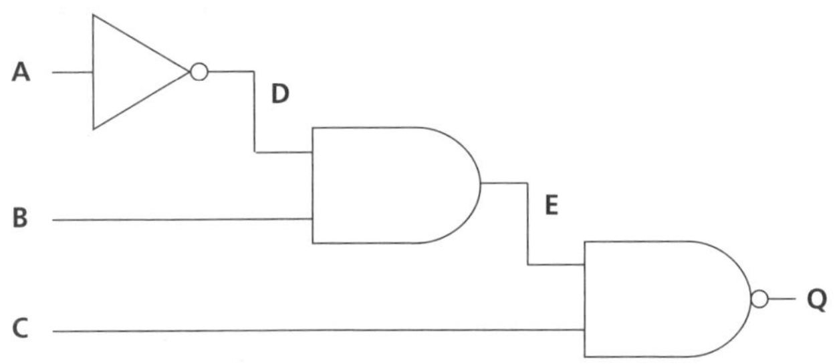

A	B	C	D	E	Q

HT

2 Another combination of logic gates is shown below. Construct the truth table for this combination of logic gates.

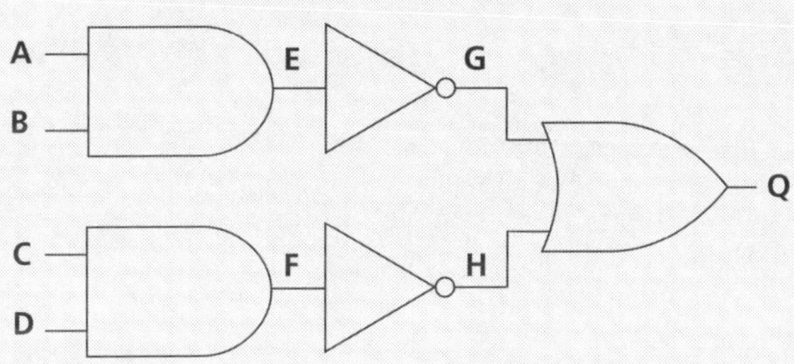

A	B	C	D	E	F	G	H	Q

Even More Logical

HT **3** Explain why a resistor is usually used in series with an LED in logic circuits.

4 **a)** What device is shown in the diagram opposite?

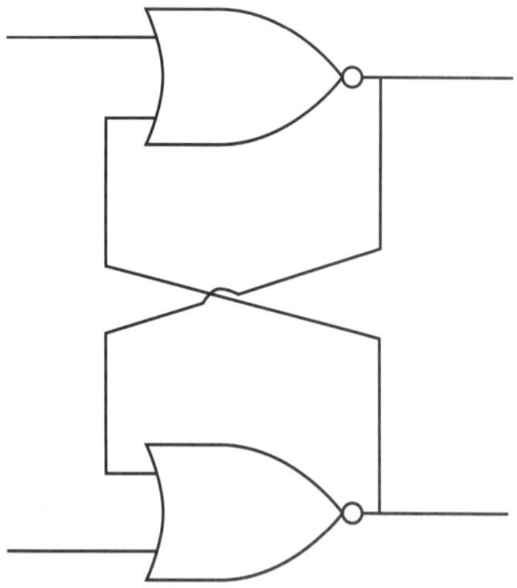

b) Why is this device useful?

HT **5** Explain why you might need a relay in a logic circuit.

6 **a)** What is a bistable latch?

b) Explain how a bistable latch works.

1 **ACROSS**

1. The maximum disturbance of a wave from a central position. (9)

4. Change in direction of a light ray as it passes from one medium to another and changes speed. (10)

6. A wave where the vibrations are at 90° to the direction of energy transfer, e.g. ripples in water. (10)

7. The distance between corresponding points on two adjacent waves. (10)

9. A push or pull acting upon an object. (5)

13. Type of energy sources that can be replaced. (9)

16. The spreading out of a wave as a result of passing an obstacle. (11)

18. The separation of light by refraction, e.g. as a result of passing through a prism. (10)

19. The energy possessed by a body due to its motion. (7)

20. The path taken by a projectile. (10)

21. A quantity where both size and direction are known. (6,8)

DOWN

2. The effect produced by waves overlapping. (12)

3. A measure of the state of motion of an object as a product of its mass and velocity. (8)

5. The energy an object has because of its mass and height above the Earth. (13,9)

8. Measure of the difference in potential between two points in an electrical circuit. (7)

10. The number of waves produced in one second. (9)

11. The blocking of light waves that oscillate in certain directions, for example, to cut out glare. (12)

12. Type of electricity that is produced by friction and does not flow. (6)

14. A quantity where size only is known. (6,8)

15. A wave where the vibrations are in the same direction as the energy transfer, e.g. the type of wave produced by pushing a spring. (12)

17. The total force acting on an object; all the forces combined. (9)

Glossary

Notes

Acknowledgements

ISBN: 978-1-906415-03-7

Published by Letts and Lonsdale.

Authors: Robert Johnson and Professor Averil Macdonald
Project Editor: Rachael Hemsley
Cover and concept design: Sarah Duxbury
Designer: Nicola Lancashire
Artwork: Letts and Lonsdale, and HL Studios.

Letts and Lonsdale make every effort to ensure that all paper used in our books is made from wood pulp obtained from sustainable and well-managed forests.

Author Information

Robert Johnson is a full-time teacher of physics at a respected co-educational public school. He has an innovative approach towards teaching, which makes physics relevant and interesting.

Professor Averil Macdonald is Chair of Science Communication at the University of Reading. She was awarded The Bragg Medal 1999 for her distinguished contribution to physics education and Woman of Outstanding Achievement in Science 2007 for her success popularising physics.